Date: 02/02/12

J 523.46 ADA
Adamson, Thomas K.,
Saturn /

Pebble® Plus

Exploring the Galaxy
Saturn

by Thomas K. Adamson

Consulting Editor: Gail Saunders-Smith, PhD

Consultant: James Gerard
Aerospace Education Specialist, NASA
Kennedy Space Center, Florida

Capstone press®

Mankato, Minnesota

Pebble Plus is published by Capstone Press,
151 Good Counsel Drive, P.O. Box 669, Mankato, Minnesota 56002.
www.capstonepress.com

1 2 3 4 5 6 12 11 10 09 08 07

Library of Congress Cataloging-in-Publication Data
Adamson, Thomas K., 1970–
    Saturn / by Thomas K. Adamson.—Rev. and updated.
    p. cm.—(Pebble plus. Exploring the galaxy)
    Includes bibliographical references and index.
    ISBN-13: 978-1-4296-0733-9 (hardcover)
    ISBN-10: 1-4296-0733-5 (hardcover)
    1. Saturn (Planet)—Juvenile literature. I. Title. II. Series.
QB671.A32 2008
523.46—dc22   2007004455

Summary: Simple text and photographs describe the planet Saturn.

Editorial Credits
Mari C. Schuh, editor; Kia Adams, designer; Alta Schaffer, photo researcher

Photo Credits
Digital Vision, 5 (Venus), 9, 10–11
NASA, 5 (Jupiter); JPL/Caltech, 5 (Uranus); JPL/Space Science Institute, 12–13
PhotoDisc Inc., cover, 4 (Neptune); 5 (Mars, Mercury, Sun, Saturn, Earth), 17 (both); Stock Trek, 1, 14–15; PhotoDisc Imaging, 7
Photo Researchers Inc./Jerry Lodriguss, 21
Photri-Microstock, 19

Note: Some of the images in this book are false-color images that use artificial colors to enhance planet features.

Note to Parents and Teachers

The Exploring the Galaxy set supports national science standards related to earth science. This book describes and illustrates the planet Saturn. The photographs support early readers in understanding the text. The repetition of words and phrases helps early readers learn new words. This book also introduces early readers to subject-specific vocabulary words, which are defined in the Glossary section. Early readers may need assistance to read some words and to use the Table of Contents, Glossary, Read More, Internet Sites, and Index sections of the book.

Table of Contents

Saturn

Saturn is the sixth planet
from the Sun.
Saturn is the
second largest planet
in the solar system.

The Solar System

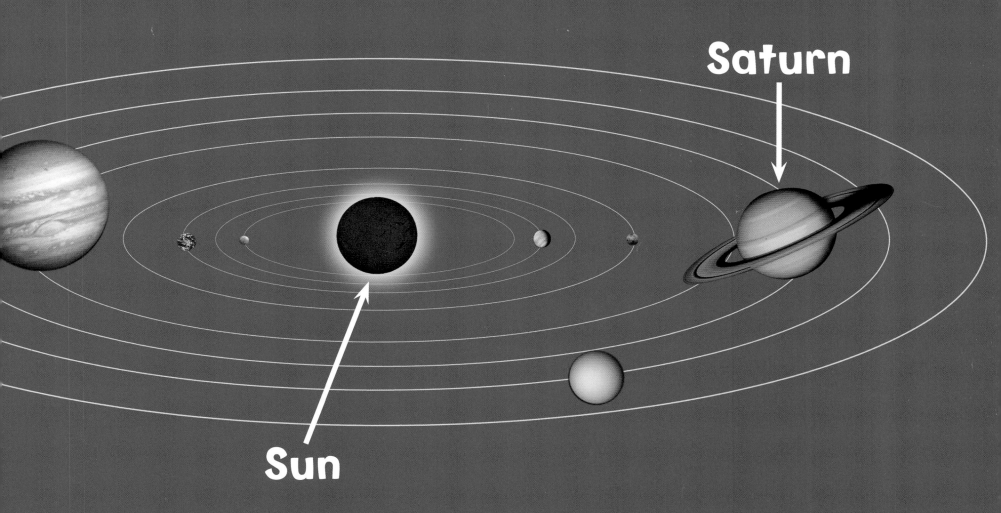

Saturn

Sun

Saturn is a ball
of gases and clouds.
Saturn is called
a gas giant.

Thick clouds cover Saturn.

Saturn does not have

a solid surface.

Spacecrafts cannot

land on Saturn.

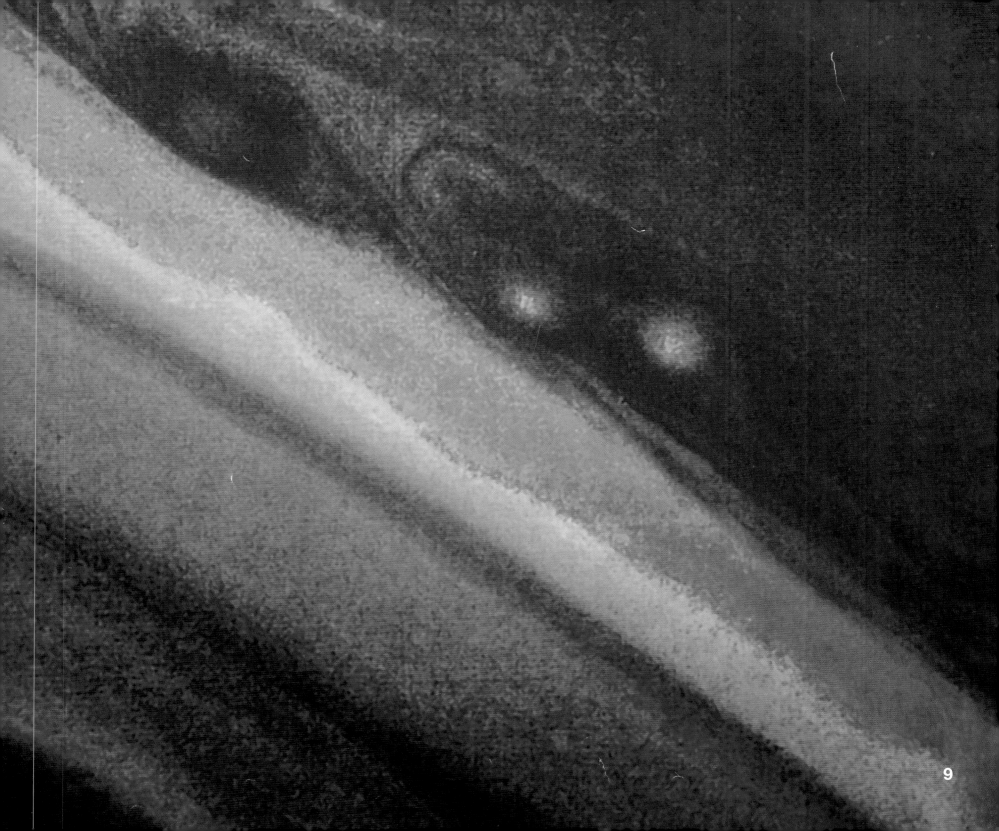

9

At least 31 moons
move around Saturn.
Earth has only one moon.

Saturn's Rings

Saturn's rings
are wide and flat.
People on Earth
can see the rings
with a telescope.

Saturn's rings are pieces
of rock and ice.
Some pieces are
as big as a car.

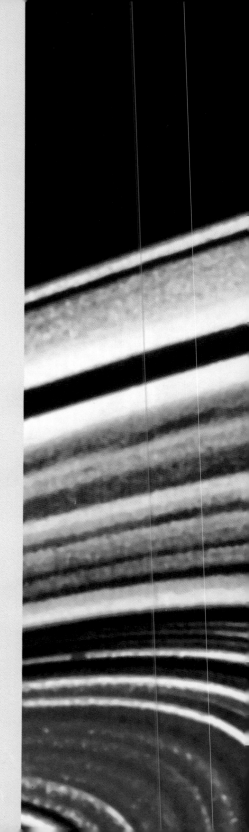

Saturn's Size

Saturn and its rings
are almost 10 times
wider than Earth.

Earth

Saturn

People and Saturn

It is too cold for people

to live on Saturn.

The air is so cold on Saturn

that people cannot breathe.

People can see Saturn
from Earth.
Saturn looks like
a bright star.

Saturn

Glossary

gas—a substance, such as air, that spreads to fill any space that holds it; Saturn is mostly made of gases.

moon—an object that moves around a planet

planet—a large object that moves around the Sun; Saturn is the sixth planet from the Sun; there are eight planets in the solar system.

solar system—the Sun and the objects that move around it; our solar system has eight planets, dwarf planets including Pluto, and many moons, asteroids, and comets.

spacecraft—a vehicle used to travel in space

star—a large ball of burning gases in space; the Sun is a star.

Sun—the star that the planets move around; the Sun provides light and heat to the planets.

surface—the outside or outermost area of something

telescope—a tool people use to look at planets and other objects in space

Read More

Orme, Helen, and David Orme. *Let's Explore Saturn*. Space Launch! Milwaukee: Gareth Stevens, 2007.

Richardson, Adele. *Saturn*. First Facts: The Solar System. Mankato, Minn.: Capstone Press, 2008.

Wimmer, Teresa. *Saturn*. My First Look at Planets. Mankato, Minn.: Creative Education, 2007.

Internet Sites

FactHound offers a safe, fun way to find Internet sites related to this book. All of the sites on FactHound have been researched by our staff.

Here's how:

1. Visit *www.facthound.com*

2. Choose your grade level.

3. Type in this book ID **1429607335** for age-appropriate sites. You may also browse subjects by clicking on letters, or by clicking on pictures and words.

4. Click on the **Fetch It** button.

FactHound will fetch the best sites for you!

Index

Word Count: 136
Grade: 1
Early-Intervention Level: 14